Scottish Inspirations
Edited by Michelle Afford

Young**Writers**

First published in Great Britain in 2007 by:
Young Writers
Remus House
Coltsfoot Drive
Peterborough
PE2 9JX
Telephone: 01733 890066
Website: www.youngwriters.co.uk

SB ISBN 978-1 84431 235 1

Foreword

Young Writers was established in 1991 and has been passionately devoted to the promotion of reading and writing in children and young adults ever since. The quest continues today. Young Writers remains as committed to the nurturing of poetic and literary talent as ever.

This year's Young Writers competition has proven as vibrant and dynamic as ever and we are delighted to present a showcase of the best poetry from across the UK and in some cases overseas. Each poem has been selected from a wealth of *Little Laureates* entries before ultimately being published in this, our sixteenth primary school poetry series.

Once again, we have been supremely impressed by the overall quality of the entries we have received. The imagination, energy and creativity which has gone into each young writer's entry made choosing the poems a challenging and often difficult but ultimately hugely rewarding task - the general high standard of the work submitted ensured this opportunity to bring their poetry to a larger appreciative audience.

We sincerely hope you are pleased with this final collection and that you will enjoy *Little Laureates Scottish Inspirations* for many years to come.

Contents

Auchencairn School, Castle Douglas
Oriel Marshall (10)   19

Birkhill Primary School, Birkhill
Ellen Stewart (7)   20
Jack Taylor (7)   21
Jade Crawford (7)   21
Adam Gill (7)   21
Isla Cameron (7)   22
Sam Hodgson (8)   22
Jonathan Duffy (8)   22
Tom Roussel (8)   23
Martin George (8)   23
Charlotte Robertson (8)   23
Kerren Jollands (8)   24
Alessia Di Ponio (8)   24
Kirsten Ferrier (8)   24
Calum Findleton (8)   25
Myles Storrier (8)   25
Douglas Salmond (7)   25
Aaron Thomson (9)   26
Rachael Scrimgeour (9)   26
Eleanor Williams (9)   26
Anya Davidson (9)   27
Cormac Nicoll (10)   27
Blair Doughty (9)   27
Rachel George (9)   28
Glen Merry (9)   28
Anna Brown (9)   28
Catriona Strachan (10)   29
Lorna Maxwell Carroll (10)   29
Aaron Barnes (9)   29
Jamie Powell (10)   30
Calum Anderson (10)   30
Joshua Boyd (10)   30
Kyle Morrison (9)   31
Arran MacDonald (10)   31
Scott Walker (9)   31
Scott Mitchell (9)   32
Amy Doogan (11)   32
David Milne (9)   33

Blackhall Primary School, Edinburgh

Vincent Plummer (9)	49
Grant McDonell (10)	49
Laura Burt (10)	50
Alex Larionov (9)	50
Campbell Orr (9)	51

Chapel of Garloch Primary School, Inverurie
Jessica Smith (8)	51
Daniel McNally (7)	51
Dani Donald (8)	52
Beth Strachan (10)	52
Ellen Robertson (9)	53
Kate Fowler (10)	53
Tanya Gill (10)	54
Bridie Pryce (9)	54
Michael Walls (9)	55
Jordan Ramsay (8)	55
Kirsty Smith (9)	56
Rebecca Fyfe (9)	57

Edinburgh Academy Junior School, Edinburgh
Benjamin Wong (10)	57
Barney Withall (11)	58
Bill Thompson (10)	58
Marc Petrie (10)	58
Ben Brown (10)	59
Finn Macpherson (10)	59
Rory Hardie (10)	59
Ross Millican (11)	60
Ruaridh Gale (11)	60
Nathaniel Brailsford (10)	60
Patrick Paterson (11)	61
John Smyth (10)	61

Flora Stevenson Primary School, Edinburgh
Azeem Nabi (8)	61
Alix Taylor (9)	62
Peter Robertson (8)	62
Michael Keegan (8)	62
Cara Targett-Ness (10)	63

Jamie Penman (12)	86
Aimee Hynd (11)	87
Jennifer Cope (9)	87
Micaela Brown (11)	88
Liam Sloan (12)	88
Amy Barbour (11)	89
Kyle Thomson (12)	89
Phoebe Barbour	90
Zoe Drury (11)	90
Zoe Cook (9)	91
Sarah Pettiglio (11)	91
Alice Eve Roberts (9)	92
Ross Galloway Stuart (9)	92
Lindsay Smith (9)	93
Kelsey Lenaghan (9)	93
Catriona Kirk (9)	94
Kiera Hynd (9)	94
Laura Mackenzie (9)	95
Claire Douglas (11)	95
Chloe Sandilands (9)	96
Megan Lister (9)	97
Lauren Howitt (9)	98
Amy Deas (9)	99

St Andrew's Primary School, Fraserburgh

Kristofer Maitland (8)	99
Marc Busby (9)	100
Isla Sutherland (8)	100
Holly Milne (8)	101
Ross Lawrence (8)	101
Nicole Ritchie (9)	102
Lara Reid (9)	102
Stephanie Cardno (9)	103
Chelsea Wilkinson (9)	103
Craig Massie (8)	104
Brad Lockyer (9)	104
Carrie Scott (8)	105
Shaun Muir (9)	105
Liam Maitland (9)	106
Meagan Ewing (8)	106
Claire Smith (9)	107

Sgoil Staoinebrig, Stoneybridge

The Poems

The Magic Box

(Based on 'Magic Box' by Kit Wright)

I will put in the box . . .
petals from a red rose,
stones from a deep sea,
diamonds from the deepest mines.

I will put in the box . . .
the first flower to bloom in spring,
raindrops on a red rose,
picture of a great memory.

I will put in the box . . .
feather from a peacock,
a stream running through the forest,
my first word.

I will put in the box . . .
wet sand from the sea,
the voice of an angel,
the last snowflake of the year.

My box is fashioned from
flowers, rubies and raindrops from the sky,
with angels on the lid and stars in the corners.

Katie Park (10)

The Rainforest

R ainy and hot
A nimals galore
I nnocent prey
N ever-ending growth
F orever living
O r might just die if chopping continues
R ot the trees
E nough animals to fill the country
S ave the trees for
T he best place in the world.

Matthew Ross (9)

Death Or Life

I'm in bed resting my weary head.
I close my eyes. Oh, what's this?
I'm in the clouds, flying high and feeling proud.

I'm a blue tit,
A blue tit with a beautiful blue cap
And a bright yellow breast.
My head has a wavy streak
Beneath the blue and black strip
Shooting out from my eye.

Oh no, here comes a bird.
It's enormous with wings so long and so wide.
Oh my gosh, it's fast. It's a falcon.
I'm done for.

I have to hide, but where?
There's a bird box,
I'll fly inside or I will die,
That's for sure.

What's that?
Beep . . . beep . . . beep, beep, beep.

I'm awake,
I'm in my bed. No wings, legs instead.
I'm not dead.

It was a dream.

Claire Barnes-Miller (9)
Achfary Primary School, Achfary

Dinosaur Dream

I was in a big forest of palm trees.

I looked up,
The leaves were huge,
Like giant green tiles on a roof.
I knocked the palm tree,
Coconuts fell on my head.
I fell to the ground,
They gave me a headache.
I stood up,
I staggered into a grey giant thing.
I did not know what to do.
I looked up.

It was massive,
It was an apatosaurus,
I couldn't believe my eyes.

I thought dinosaurs were extinct.

I heard a loud call,
I recognised that noise.
It was a tyrannosaurus.

The apatosaurus said to me, 'Are you okay kid?'
I couldn't believe my ears,
I didn't think dinosaurs could talk.

Kelly Spence (8)
Achfary Primary School, Achfary

War

The troops are running in a manic dash,
Driven by the force inside them
To save their wives, their children, their nation.
Horses with wide bloodshot eyes gallop past,
Spurred on by the spiked boots of the knights.
Enemy knights charge,
Hacking men down, disemboweling, decapitating mindlessly.
Swords flash in the sunlight, swords stained with blood.
Their faces, covered in steel helmets, have no mercy.
The clashing noise of sword on sword fills the soldiers' ears,
Deafening them with the roar of battle.

One side is regrouping.
Each death spurring them on to avenge their fallen friends,
To charge the enemy with their halberds, to kill them all.
Every injury, mutilation and death encourages
The flaming hatred of the enemy.
A massive battalion of knights charges,
The archers of the enemy fire at the knights, driving them back.
The last strength of the enemy is exhausted.
Turning, the knights flee.

The land is safe. Victory is claimed,
But it is victory with sadness, many brave men lie dead,
Victims of the foul craft of war.

Patrick Gray (10)
Achfary Primary School, Achfary

Maybe

I don't need crisps or sweets when I come home from school.
Mrs Adam, our school cook, makes incredibly good food,
Especially cheesy pasta, my favourite.

When I've walked home from school,
I choose my spot in the living room, where there is peace and quiet.

My Game Boy is set up,
My index fingers and thumbs are ready to play.
It's very hard, but I like it.
I really want to catch Mew and Mewtwo,
They are very powerful.

I don't know how long it will take,
Maybe five weeks, maybe more.
One day I will say I've completed it.
Maybe I'll be powerful.
Maybe I'll be a trainer in the game.
Maybe I'll be the best trainer in all the games ever.
Maybe.

Callum Amos (7)
Achfary Primary School, Achfary

Night.

Night runs down the path
And round the corner
Into the street where Sun still stands.
The owl is flying
As a pool of darkness spreads.
Night is using his dark powers
To make Day fall asleep.
At last he has won and has control
Over the world for now.

Scott Black (10)
Applegrove Primary School, Forres

Night's Friends

Night is a big, dark lake
Like a spy, he spies on the sun.
When the sun is sleepy, he puts day to bed.
Night climbs out of the dark lake
And puts a dark blanket over the world.
He sails through the dark blanket,
Sticking on golden stars to stand out
So someone can see.
He goes over to the moon
And makes the light on the moon.
When the animals see this,
Some go to bed and some come out.
The bats and owls come out to play,
And are the night's friends.
Night walks through the town.
The lights come on as if he were a king.
Day has gone to bed,
But Night has arrived.

Sarah Williams (11)
Applegrove Primary School, Forres

Night

Night floats in on the dark, calm sea,
Swimming gracefully with her stars,
Putting the sun to sleep.
With the dark blanket of the night sky,
The sun falls asleep as fast as a blink.
The bats and owls start coming down
Landing on the trees in their homes.
Adults searching for food to feed their children,
Swooping through trees opposite houses,
Landing outside bins, picking up scraps
And scrambling home.
The sky goes black . . .
The sun is gone.

Chloe Allan (10)
Applegrove Primary School, Forres

Night Is Alive

Night came in
a pool of darkness
swimming up
to the shore.

He pulled a
dark curtain
all around Day
leaving her
to sleep.

He flicked up
a switch to
turn the moon on.
Glittering stars
hanging on strings.

Night was here
like a big black bat
spreading his wings
to fly.

Laura Carter (10)
Applegrove Primary School, Forres

The Pitch-Black Night

Night came in from a pool of darkness.
Her golden-star eyes looked down to the ground.
Out from a tree came a big black bat,
Flipping and turning,
Flying and swirling.
Round the corner it came,
Flying like a plane.
Down went the sun behind a hill,
Revealing the black sky,
And on came the street lights.

Bethany Welsh (10)
Applegrove Primary School, Forres

Nightlife

Night came in on a never-ending sea.
The world had gone to sleep.
She was trickling through the streets,
Turning all the lights on as she went by.
She was creeping into the houses,
Shutting all the curtains to put people to sleep.
The moon was like a bodyguard constantly looking after the sun.
The night was as black as a black cat,
With golden stars sprinkled all over it.
Night had come.

Lewis Daley (10)
Applegrove Primary School, Forres

Night

Night-time tucks Daytime to bed.
A signal is made.
Animals come out to play.
Night-time swings to the sky,
Sticking stars above.
It is a pool of darkness.
Total silence . . .
Night has come!

Josh MacPhee (10)
Applegrove Primary School, Forres

Night

Night-time rolled in like a wave in the sea.
The golden stars appeared in the dark sky.
The streetlights pinged on suddenly,
Splashing the world into silence.

Connor Sim (10)
Applegrove Primary School, Forres

Night

Night comes in
Swimming in a silent river made of living darkness.
He floats to an empty street, splashing at the afternoon.
He dives at the sky, turning it black
And sticking on stars that match the colour of his eyes.
Night floats by, awake and energetic.
Day falls asleep and changes its mind,
But Night has arrived.

Craig Reilly (11)
Applegrove Primary School, Forres

Pool Of Darkness

Night had come in a silent pool of darkness,
So he cast a spell on the sun to make it go to sleep.
He switched the sun to the moon
And pulled black curtains over the sky,
Once he had put the sun behind the curtains.
He stuck his stars on the Velcro.
Finally, Night had arrived.

Kris McInnes (10)
Applegrove Primary School, Forres

Goodnight Sun

Night came in with golden stars hovering over
Hairy black bats came out of a scary dark cave
The waves of the thick dark river
Zooming down the dark mist of mystery
The moon stretched and yawned with a smile
And in bed was Daytime.

Kyle Reaper (10)
Applegrove Primary School, Forres

The Mosset Burn

T wisting and turning,
H asty over bumps,
E ndless flowing.

M eanders put up speed,
O ver the waterfall.
S limy salmon in the water,
S ometimes there are duck races,
E ver so fast.
T he tavern can view the burn.

B ridges where you can see it,
U nderneath is very revolting!
R ocky splashes,
N o swimming allowed.

Duncan Fraser (9)
Applegrove Primary School, Forres

The Night Sky

The sun closes its eyes
behind the hill.
The moon rises with
the golden yellow stars
shining in the night sky.
All that's left is silence.
The sky is nothing
but a black sky.
A little river trickles
along down the path.
Night burns
the bright sun.

Rebecca Gordon (10)
Applegrove Primary School, Forres

Fire Dancing

Fire danced in an orange and yellow dress.
Her flame-red hair bounced on her shoulders
As she danced crazily through the houses.
Everyone tried to stop her,
But she kept on dancing,
Faster and more fiercely.
Water tried to stop her,
But he just disappeared.
More water was used,
But the Great Fire of London had begun.
She made crackling sounds.
She burnt furniture and houses to the ground.
Suddenly even more water was used.
Fire stopped, she was soaked
And her powers had gone.

Alicia Connell (10)
Applegrove Primary School, Forres

The River Findhorn

Tumbling, tumbling round and round
Flowing quickly to where we're bound
Quickly speeding round the bend
Will this journey ever end?

Gliding gracefully to the sea
Never stopping, not even for some tea
Splashing, splashing all the way
To get to where the sea will lay.

Speeding quickly over rocks
At the speed of adult hawks
Splashing gently in the sea
What's my destination going to be?

Miriam Scott (9)
Applegrove Primary School, Forres

Water

On a huge waterfall,
With no water, then,
He comes gushing over the top,
Falling and splashing into the empty ditch,
He lands with a big splash,
He swims and glides in the ditch,
Filling it with water,
He brings life to everything
Then, all of a sudden, he crashes
Into a wide, deep river,
He moves slowly now,
He lurks in the darkness,
Always moving forward, never backward.

Ted Collins (11)
Applegrove Primary School, Forres

Fire

Fire attacks a pile of sticks,
He holds onto the bark and eats his way through,
He burns on and on,
He dances round his enemy and roars,
He feeds on and attacks another pile,
He leaves behind part of his body,
He blazes and spins his fiery red cape,
He grasps his foe with intense hands,
The trees scream as they are seized,
Leaving only one thing behind,
Ash!

Lawrence Clark (11)
Applegrove Primary School, Forres

Rainbow

Rain thundering down,
Sun shining bright,
I conjure up a fairy flight,

Ruby, Amber, Saffron,
Fern, Sky, Inky, Heather,
Fairies of the rainbow,

Seven beautiful streams of colour,
Dancing in the sky,
Laughing, playing,

As the days go by,
Fading away and away,
As the storm fades into the distance,

Then it's peaceful,
And calm, but no
Rainbow.

Chloe Watson (10)
Applegrove Primary School, Forres

Snow

Snow comes rushing through the sky,
Driving rain and clouds away,
She has a beautiful white skirt and jacket,
Sprinkling snow on the ground,
Swirling in the sky,
Everybody wakes up to a white morning,
Snow dashes around corners,
Then runs away for another year.

Lisa Sutherland (10)
Applegrove Primary School, Forres

r Helpful Friend Night

Night swoops in
holding a rucksack.
He takes out of that rucksack
a blanket as black as a bat.
He puts the blanket over Day
and tucks her into sleep
then he moves on.
Now he takes out a switch
he turns it on
the moon comes out
followed by his brothers and sisters.
His movements are like mice.
He soars and swoops
for hours and hours
until there is a yawn.
Day has woken up.
He puts everything back in his rucksack
and slithers to the other side of the world in a moment.

Rachel Fraser (11)
Applegrove Primary School, Forres

The Mosset Burn

M oving fast
O ver stones
S trong current
S eals singing
E ast forward
T wisting round

B umbly rocks
U nnoticeable fish
R ocks rocking
N ever stopping.

Daniel Sutherland (9)
Applegrove Primary School, Forres

Night-Time

The sun closes its eyes
And the moon takes its place.
Night turns the bright sky
Into a pool of darkness.
Night wakens the night-time animals
With his silence.
He puts the stars in the sky
With his wind-like breath.
Night makes the moon come out
By making the sun disappear.
This is Night.
He has come to play.

Kirsty McBeath (10)
Applegrove Primary School, Forres

The Night Ninja

Night comes through the world
As quick as a ninja
Leaving a shroud of darkness behind it.
He charges round once more
Putting stars in the darkness.
As he finishes the job
He opens the gates withholding the night creatures.
Then he returns to the house
Making sure the day ninja is asleep.
For the rest of the night
He will help and protect the night creatures.

Kieran Sharp (10)
Applegrove Primary School, Forres

Lightning

Dark clouds covered the sky,
Rain was falling down,
An enormous *bang!*
Then a streak of light,
It was me and Thunder,
Scaring everyone in sight,
Scaring the sun away,
It was a lovely day
Before the sun went away,
Then the dark clouds faded away,
The rain stopped,
Then we went away.

Jade Fawcett (10)
Applegrove Primary School, Forres

Snow

Snow came in
On a frosty morning,
Falling from the sky,
Tap-tapping on the window,
All was white,
She was glad,
She flew across
The big black sky.

Eilish Cunningham (10)
Applegrove Primary School, Forres

Snow

She came blowing from the north,
Wearing a white snowflake skirt,
Flowing everywhere,
Blowing in everyone's faces,
She wore a long, shiny top,
White hair surrounded her white face,
I could feel her gushing onto my skin,
She felt strange and prickly,
Then everything stopped and went silent,
She returned to the North Pole,
I'm sure she will be back next year.

Elaine Munro (10)
Applegrove Primary School, Forres

Dinosaurs

D inosaurs are wonderful pets.
 I   have one myself.
N ever ever do they bite you and they don't make a mess.
O ver in the corner of my room there he sits in the gloom.
S itting on the carpet he eats and sleeps all day.
A nd you should listen to all the things my friends say.
U gly he is not, but my cousin says so.
R onnie is just jealous, that's what I know.
S o me and my dinosaur have lots and lots of fun.

Linzi Fraser (8)
Applegrove Primary School, Forres

Night Spy

Night comes in
On a never-ending sea
Sneaking up on Daytime
Like a dark spy.

The moon is like a siren
Waking up the animals
Now not so silent
The night has woken.

The night puts a curtain on the world
The moon guards the darkness
Nothing can stop it now
Because Night has come.

Gordon Smart (11)
Applegrove Primary School, Forres

Midnight

As the cold sun sets,
the moon comes out
and puts the sun away to bed.
His best friend, the sun,
is always asleep in bed.
The dark pool of water
moves across the land.
The bats are woken up
by the tree.
Then it is morning,
the sun comes up
and the moon goes to bed.

Shelbie Ross (10)
Applegrove Primary School, Forres

Goldilocks And The Three Bears

Once in the woods
A long time ago,
Was a girl with gold hair
That would shine and flow.

She came to a house
And opened the door,
And there was a table
On the old wooden floor.

And there on the table
Were three bowls of porridge,
She was very hungry
She had not learnt to forage.

She did try the first
Hot, hot, boiling hot!
The second, too cold
Too long out of the pot.

The third was just right
Yum-yum, it was great!
She finished it all
None left on the plate.

She looked all around
And saw some old stairs,
She ran right to the top
And there were three chairs.

The first was too hard
Made of solid wood,
The second, too soft
It flopped down like a hood.

The third was just right
Like it was her own,
But she heard a *crackkk!*
And it broke with a groan.

She ran into the bedroom
And three beds she saw,
She was very tired
She had been sweeping the floor.

She lay down on the first,
Too hard, *ouch, ouch, ouch!*
She lay on the second
Too soft like a couch.

The third was just right
It fitted like a glove,
She did snore very loud
You could hear in the heavens above.

Meanwhile in the woods
Three bears were coming back,
They were coming back home
To their little shack.

They did run up the stairs
Saw Goldie lying there,
When the little bear saw her
He fell in love with her gold hair.

They did get married
And oh, what a show!
A girl and bear married
A very long time ago.

Oriel Marshall (10)
Auchencairn School, Castle Douglas

Darkness

Darkness is black like an old lady's cat
It sounds like thunder
It smells like disgusting goo
It looks like you
It makes me sick
It reminds me of a brick.

Ellen Stewart (7)
Birkhill Primary School, Birkhill

Anger

Anger sounds like an eagle screaming to its death.
Anger tastes like blood running down your clothes.
Anger smells like the lava out of a volcano going up your nose.
Anger looks like an old man stamping his foot for no reason.
Anger feels like you're holding a dead body.
Anger reminds me of a man with a spear, smashing it into the ice.

Jack Taylor (7)
Birkhill Primary School, Birkhill

Anger

Anger is red like an exploding volcano.
It sounds like a bomb going off in a meadow.
It tastes like ashes and fire and smoke.
It smells like blood and someone dying.
It looks like someone dying in pain.
It feels like you are being stabbed in the back.
It reminds me of one of the worst days in my life.

Jade Crawford (7)
Birkhill Primary School, Birkhill

Darkness

Darkness is black like a zombie in a graveyard.
Darkness tastes like a dead man.
Darkness feels like a ghost in the sky.
Darkness looks like a vampire.
Darkness smells like blood.
Darkness reminds me of a zombie.

Adam Gill (7)
Birkhill Primary School, Birkhill

Hate

Hate makes me think of an exploding volcano, all red
and so powerful.
It tastes like blood in your mouth.
It smells like smelly old breath.
It looks like a very old witch.
It feels like someone's old skin.
It reminds me of an old lady.

Isla Cameron (7)
Birkhill Primary School, Birkhill

Love

Love is red and it is like blossom flying down from the sky.
Love sounds like birds singing.
Love tastes like a box of chocolates.
Love smells like red roses.
Love looks like love hearts.
Love feels nice.
Love reminds me of my cat.

Sam Hodgson (8)
Birkhill Primary School, Birkhill

Darkness

Darkness is red like your own cut.
It sounds like a tap leaking.
It tastes like rotten eggs.
It smells like rotten feet.
It looks like a dark cloud.
It feels like witches' teeth.
It reminds me of when I am all alone.

Jonathan Duffy (8)
Birkhill Primary School, Birkhill

Sadness

Sadness is red like a dead man's head.
It sounds like a forest being chopped down.
It smells like a burning fire.
It tastes like a cup of blood.
It looks like a person being stabbed in the head.
It feels like a person screaming for help.

Tom Roussel (8)
Birkhill Primary School, Birkhill

Fun

Fun sounds like splashing in water in summer.
It tastes like eating fruit kebabs.
Fun smells like blossom falling off a tree.
Fun looks like a clown dancing.
It feels like smooth flower petals.
It reminds me of the summer.

Martin George (8)
Birkhill Primary School, Birkhill

Love

Love sounds like the waves in the ocean.
Love tastes like strawberry tarts with cream.
Love smells like dark chocolate.
Love looks like two joining hearts.
Love feels like soft and cuddly pillows.
Love reminds me of my cute dog.

Charlotte Robertson (8)
Birkhill Primary School, Birkhill

Happiness

Happiness is orange and tastes like sweet, sweet honey.
Happiness lives in the heart of God.
It sounds like friends running to you to give you presents
                                              and soft love too.
It smells like roses in line waiting just for you.
It looks like sand giving you little sparkles.
It feels like me hugging angels and, most of all, loving
                                              loving each other.

Kerren Jollands (8)
Birkhill Primary School, Birkhill

Fun

Fun is so yellow like a sun in the sky.
Fun always tastes like a butterfly flying by.
Fun always smells like a rose in a bush.
Fun always looks like a very fun park.
Fun makes me feel like I have love inside.
Fun makes me remember a really fun time.

Alessia Di Ponio (8)
Birkhill Primary School, Birkhill

Fun

Fun is red like a bouncy bed.
Fun looks like a red roller coaster.
Fun sounds like a bear laughing.
Fun tastes like melting chocolate.
Fun reminds me of a red flower.
Fun feels like a talking bear.
Fun smells like red roses.

Kirsten Ferrier (8)
Birkhill Primary School, Birkhill

Fun

Fun sounds like a fairy in the sky.
Fun tastes like a lollipop going down your throat.
Fun smells like perfume being sprayed.
Fun looks like clouds dancing in the sky.
Fun feels like swinging on a swing.
Fun reminds me of my grandad when I was one year old but he died!

Calum Findleton (8)
Birkhill Primary School, Birkhill

Anger

Anger is red like a dead man's chest.
It tastes like red blood too.
It sounds like a man shouting.
It smells like a muddy black cat.
It feels like a rough elephant.
It reminds me of a dead skeleton.

Myles Storrier (8)
Birkhill Primary School, Birkhill

Darkness

Darkness is black like a rumble in a cave.
Darkness tastes like blood from a vampire's mouth.
It smells like a breath from a witch.
It looks like a dark castle at night.
It feels like stinky witches' feet.
It reminds me of when my sister scared me.

Douglas Salmond (7)
Birkhill Primary School, Birkhill

Sadness

Sadness is black like a dungeon in a castle.
Sadness sounds like someone being killed.
It smells like a city burning down.
Sadness looks like lightning on a rainy day.
Sadness feels like a thorn bush ripping through your flesh.
Sadness reminds me of someone in my family who has died.
It tastes like dirt from fields.

Aaron Thomson (9)
Birkhill Primary School, Birkhill

Laughter

Laughter is colourful and bright like the sun.
It feels like a fluffy blanket.
It tastes like a big bowl of strawberry ice cream.
It sounds like children laughing in a park.
Laughter smells like a big breath of fresh air.
Laughter looks like the playground on a sunny day.
Laughter reminds me of being younger, running and laughing
around with my friends.

Rachael Scrimgeour (9)
Birkhill Primary School, Birkhill

Anger

Anger is red like a ball of fire.
It sounds like thunder striking a tree.
Anger tastes like curry - flaming hot.
It smells like smoke all around me.
It looks like lava spilling out of a volcano.
Anger feels like blood oozing out of my knee.
Anger reminds me of war - I don't like it!

Eleanor Williams (9)
Birkhill Primary School, Birkhill

Hate

Hate is black like a stormy night.
It tastes like horrible liquorice coming out of your mouth.
Hate sounds like someone screaming.
It smells like someone who's never cleaned their teeth.
Hate looks like a teacher on a bad day.
It feels like someone stabbing you in the back.
Hate reminds me of when I split up with my best friends.

Anya Davidson (9)
Birkhill Primary School, Birkhill

Love

Love is light pink,
Like a pink flamingo.
It sounds like happy people.
Love tastes like love heart sweeties.
Love smells like candyfloss.
It looks like somebody's heart beating.
Love feels like soft marshmallows.
Love reminds me of hot melted cheese.

Cormac Nicoll (10)
Birkhill Primary School, Birkhill

Fear

Fear is blue like the sky that keeps changing.
It tastes like a dead deer.
Fear looks like a scared rabbit.
It sounds like a shaking bin.
Fear feels like a cold person.
It reminds me of a soaking building.

Blair Doughty (9)
Birkhill Primary School, Birkhill

Sadness

Sadness is the colour red, like blood drops dripping from cuts.
Sadness sounds like earth being thrown over a coffin.
It tastes like drops from your eyes dripping down to your mouth.
Sadness smells like a skunk about to explode.
It looks like people starving on the other side of the world.
Sadness feels like someone I know being buried.
It reminds me of when somebody I know is in hospital.

Rachel George (9)
Birkhill Primary School, Birkhill

Love

Love is red like blood from a cut.
Love feels like a heart beating fast in your tummy.
It tastes like sweets waiting to be eaten.
It reminds me of Christmas Day with lots of colourful parcels.
Love sounds like church bells on a Sunday morning.
Love looks like people having fun.
It smells like candyfloss, pink, sticky and soft.

Glen Merry (9)
Birkhill Primary School, Birkhill

Fear

Fear is black like a stone in a graveyard.
It smells like an ogre when it does not wash.
Fear looks like a room with nobody in it.
It reminds me of a stormy night.
Fear feels like a brick falling on me.
It tastes like Brussels sprouts at Christmas.
Fear sounds like a tiger roaring.

Anna Brown (9)
Birkhill Primary School, Birkhill

Love

Love is red like a beautiful rose.
It reminds me of a secret that nobody knows.
It tastes like marshmallows in a fondue,
It smells like very tasty chocolate mousse.
Love looks like a butterfly with patterns on its wings,
It sounds like a bird when it sings.
It feels warm and cosy like coffee or tea,
All nice and hot, ready for me.

Catriona Strachan (10)
Birkhill Primary School, Birkhill

Love

Love is red like the red of candyfloss.
It feels like fluffy pillows all red and soft.
Love tastes like sweets ready to be eaten.
It sounds like a heart pumping for love.
It smells like a tablet being made.
Love looks like people receiving roses from others.
It reminds me of when I'm hungry, eating food.

Lorna Maxwell Carroll (10)
Birkhill Primary School, Birkhill

Hate

Hate is black like a black hole.
It smells like a person who has not cleaned their teeth.
Hate sounds like a man shouting out loud.
Hate tastes like a bottle of hot chilli sauce.
It looks like a black room.
It reminds me of a night sky.
It feels like a hard elephant.

Aaron Barnes (9)
Birkhill Primary School, Birkhill

Anger

Anger is fiery red like a volcano exploding.
It sounds like when I am in a bad temper, like a big fire.
Anger tastes like rotten pizza - it is so disgusting.
It smells like rotten fish exploding in your car.
Anger looks like exploding fireworks up high.
Anger looks like a red-hot gas fire burning your hands.
Anger reminds me of a big fight I was in.

Jamie Powell (10)
Birkhill Primary School, Birkhill

Hate

Hate is black like the night sky.
It sounds like a volcano erupting.
It looks like a huge black hole.
Hate feels like sadness.
Hate smells like a bag of rubbish.
It tastes like nothing.
It reminds me of darkness.

Calum Anderson (10)
Birkhill Primary School, Birkhill

Sadness

Sadness is black like an empty room.
Sadness tastes like a piece of rubbish.
Sadness smells like a bin.
Sadness feels like someone punishing you.
Sadness reminds me of death.

Joshua Boyd (10)
Birkhill Primary School, Birkhill

Laughter!

Laughter is pink like the colour of my sink,
Laughter reminds me of the great times I had with my friends,
Laughter feels like happiness in the air,
Laughter tastes like sherbet tickling in my mouth,
Laughter sounds like people having a great time,
Laughter smells like fizzy drinks,
Laughter is just fun.

Kyle Morrison (9)
Birkhill Primary School, Birkhill

Anger

Anger is black like a dead tree.
It tastes like mini filler burgers.
It smells like a rotten apple.
It looks like a dead animal.
A rotten cake.
A dead bird.
Anger reminds me of a dead tree.

Arran MacDonald (10)
Birkhill Primary School, Birkhill

Countries

There are an awful lot,
And some of them are very hot,
Each country has a flag,
And comes with a special tag.
There are one hundred and ninety-four,
So, please enter the global door.

Scott Walker (9)
Birkhill Primary School, Birkhill

Fear

Fear is brown,
like mud on the ground.
It feels shaky,
like bugs that you've found.
Fear looks ugly,
like bad-looking boys.
Fear smells bad,
like bathtub toys.
Fear reminds me of when I was scared,
like a five-year-old.
It sounds all funny,
like an object that's been sold.
It tastes ancient,
like an adult that's old.

Scott Mitchell (9)
Birkhill Primary School, Birkhill

Twinkle, Twinkle

Twinkle, twinkle little car,
I want to travel really far,
Maybe Belgium, maybe France,
I think I should take my chance.

Twinkle, twinkle little car,
I haven't travelled very far,
Maybe I'm in Aviemore,
But after that walk I'm really sore!

Twinkle, twinkle little car,
I don't think I should travel far,
My legs are sore, my feet are cold,
After that walk I'm feeling old!

Amy Doogan (11)
Birkhill Primary School, Birkhill

Wings
(Inspired by 'If I Had Wings' by Pie Corbett)

If I had wings
I would fly up to Jupiter
as fast as a rocket, very, very high.

If I had wings
I would blend into the shiny blue sky
and shout, 'Look at me, I can fly!'

If I had wings
I would say hello to all the birds
and beam like the yellow sun.

If I had wings
I would bring happiness to people's hearts
and show off my lovely wings.

David Milne (9)
Birkhill Primary School, Birkhill

Rainbow Trout

R ainbow trout have outstanding scales
A nd stomachs.
I now know
N ot far
B elow the sea,
O ily trout are
W aiting for you

T here. You start
R unning, then swimming to see them,
O ver a rock,
U nder some seaweed,
T rout lurk everywhere.

Calum (8)
Birkhill Primary School, Birkhill

Princess Cinquains

Princess
Long hair flowing
Loving, caring, kind, sweet
Going to the balls at night-times
So sad.

Princess
Golden long hair
Having lots of money
Sharing it with the poor people,
Kind, sweet.

Nicole Grieve (11)
Birkhill Primary School, Birkhill

My Cat Cinquain

My cat
He is Felix
Running away from me
Up on the roof he goes away
Felix.

Rory Lawson (11)
Birkhill Primary School, Birkhill

Dragon Cinquain

Dragon
Vicious and cruel
He's destroyed our village
Scary, scaly, with fiery breath
We grieve.

Lisa Hands (11)
Birkhill Primary School, Birkhill

Cinquains

Far East,
Lovely cities,
Cool turbans, fun to wear,
People always nice to talk to,
Iran.

Iraq,
Lovely cities,
But torn to shreds by war.
We hope this war ends very soon,
Poor East.

Jamie Scanlan (11)
Birkhill Primary School, Birkhill

Fish Cinquain

Bubbles
Bang into glass
They blow them all the time
Happy thoughts in my tank they think
Golden.

Lindsay Diane Graham (10)
Birkhill Primary School, Birkhill

Ogre Cinquain

Ogre
Massive creature
Turns things to rot and bones
Dangerous to keep as a pet
Kills loads.

Walter MacAulay (10)
Birkhill Primary School, Birkhill

World War II Cinquains

Hitler
Hated the Jews
Created Nazi band
He shot his wife then himself too
Lost war.

Prisoners
Concentration
Hunger, no food, killed them
Shower of gas not hot water
Flesh, bones.

Freedom
End of World War
Britain won the battle
Some of the Germans surrendered
World peace.

Lewis Brown (10)
Birkhill Primary School, Birkhill

Environment Cinquains

Nature,
Very urgent,
Must do something right now,
Greenpeace tries to stop the madness,
Help now.

Help by,
Putting food out,
So animals won't starve,
Whatever happens, don't give up,
Help them.

Calum MacDonald (11)
Birkhill Primary School, Birkhill

Dolphins Cinquains

Dolphins
Gracious Swimmers
Leaping from the water
Beautiful mammals in the sea
Happy?

Dolphins
Going too soon
Polluters polluting
We're taking them out of the sea
Not good.

Dolphins
Get caught in nets
Look happy but they're not
Endangered species of the sea
Extinct?

Taylor Deborah Han (10)
Birkhill Primary School, Birkhill

Twinkle, Twinkle

Twinkle, twinkle little star,
Oh I want a little car,
I want it pink, I want it blue,
Or maybe you can give me two,
It better be fast,
So I ain't last,
Oh little star,
I want that car,
I'll travel west,
But maybe I should pass a driving test!

Eilish Glassey (11)
Birkhill Primary School, Birkhill

Collie

Collie
Soft fur, sweet nose.
She likes to jump and play.
Playful, active, funny, silly,
Crazy

Cassie,
Lazy, sleepy,
Mooching, always playful,
Caring, adoring puppy love,
So cute

Puppy,
Cute silly eyes,
Silly face, big soft nose,
Soft sweet heart, crazy and jumpy.
Puppy.

Shannon Black (11)
Birkhill Primary School, Birkhill

Kingfisher

Kingfisher in the air
Not only in the air, maybe even on the ground
But he spends most of his time scanning the water
For trout, fish or anything he sees
Floating in the water
Swooping around
He catches a fish and in the end he lands on a log
He looks to the right
He looks to the left
To check there are no predators.

Blair Duncan (8)
Birkhill Primary School, Birkhill

Through That Door

Through that door
Is a jungle so tall
The leaves falling slowly
The flowers quite small
Where the trees are swaying
A lovely sound to hear
The sound of the crickets creaking
Through that door

Through that door
Are the fish of the sea
The colours of these creatures
An amazing sight to see
With lots of other animals
Dancing through the waves
When the sun is shining on them
They glimmer through the day
Through that door . . .

Eireann Robertson (9)
Birkhill Primary School, Birkhill

Humpty Dumpty

Humpty Dumpty sat on a chair
Humpty Dumpty lost his hair
The barber had to shave his head
Humpty Dumpty walked to his bed

Humpty Dumpty woke up at midnight
And looked in the mirror and had a big fright
The light was so bright
He couldn't believe his eyesight!

Stuart Dalzell (11)
Birkhill Primary School, Birkhill

Fun

Fun is yellow like juicy lemons,
Fun looks like going on holiday,
Fun reminds me of scoring goals from the halfway line,
Fun feels like playing the PlayStation,
Fun tastes like juicy apples that have just come out of the boxes,
Fun smells like melted chocolate just come off the hob,
Fun sounds like people laughing,
Fun is juicy chews.

Ollie Beecroft (9)
Birkhill Primary School, Birkhill

Fear

Fear is black like the stormy skies,
Fear reminds me of wolves, secrets and lies,
Fear tastes of the most rotten apple,
Fear smells like lava in a volcano,
Fear looks like fireworks out of control,
Fear sounds like booming thunder,
Fear feels like your body is on fire,
Fear is just terrifying!

Lara Maria McLoed (9)
Birkhill Primary School, Birkhill

Love

Love feels like passion flying high in the sky,
It tastes like candyfloss melting in my mouth,
It smells like ruby-red flowers lying at my doorstep,
It sounds like love songs in a secret lair,
It reminds me of all the happy times,
It looks like chocolate sundaes in a row,
Love is a beautiful thing!

Jessica Kelbie (9)
Birkhill Primary School, Birkhill

Love

Love is pink
Like a beautiful flower.
It tastes like some lovely ice cream.
It sounds like birds singing sweet, sweet songs.
It reminds me of church bells ringing.
It smells like melted chocolate with marshmallows.
It looks like leaves falling from a tree.
Love is in the air!

Saffron Eve Whyte (9)
Birkhill Primary School, Birkhill

Fun

Fun is the colour of hot, hot red,
Fun is the smell of the deep blue sea,
Fun tastes like cold ice cream,
Fun feels like the fluff of a feather,
Fun reminds me happiness,
Fun looks like a great ball,
Fun sounds like love in the air,
Fun is the one!

Emma Biggart (9)
Birkhill Primary School, Birkhill

Love

Love is passionate, love is kind.
It is in the heart.
Love does not boast.
Love always tells the truth.
Love is like flowers in your garden.
Love has no love for the Devil.
Love is so sweet.

Shauni Cook (9)
Birkhill Primary School, Birkhill

Through That Door

Through that door
Are the wolves in the wall
They take you away
To their home.

Through that door
Is the greatest jungle
In the world.

Through that door
Is the smallest ocean
On the planet.

Through that door
Is the biggest spider in the world
Spinning the biggest web ever.

That's what I saw
Through that door.

Sean Gauld (8)
Birkhill Primary School, Birkhill

My Pet

My pet is a rabbit called Roger,
Roger smells of a Jammy Dodger,
He's sometimes bossy,
He's never fussy.
He's sometimes shy,
He never flies,
His eye colour is brown,
He never ever frowns.
His food is yummy
In his tummy,
So here ends my poem,
About my chum!

Amy Elizabeth Parr (9)
Birkhill Primary School, Birkhill

Through That Door

Through that door
Is a beach with a house
That has sand as flooring
And a pile of cables and leaves for an oven
A pile of sticks for a sink
Two piles of dust for a sofa
A pile of dried mud for a rug.

Through that door
Is a school made of wood
There, where there are no classes
Instead there are lots of glasses
There is also a storage cupboard
With tills and even more rooms

Through that door
Is an ice rink
With no ice
But instead there is milk
Instead of ice skates they use Heelies
And they give you money
Instead of charging you money.

Michael Hands (8)
Birkhill Primary School, Birkhill

The Singing Flower!

One summer's day when I came out to play,
I saw a light and it gave me a fright,
I went to seek and I took a peek,
I saw a flower that sang every hour,
The flower sang, 'I am a flower and I sing every hour.
I smell like roses and I love being in posies!'

What an amazing sight to see in the light,
This beautiful flower with a magical power.
It's great to see and it belongs to me!

Amy Jessica Barnett Robertson (9)
Birkhill Primary School, Birkhill

Love

Love is red just like a rose,
Love sounds like waves swaying,
Love reminds me of happiness,
Love tastes like hot melted chocolate
With strawberries leaking with chocolate,
Love feels like happiness and peace,
Love looks like a great love heart,
Love smells like strawberries,
     I love love!

Amy Corstorphine (9)
Birkhill Primary School, Birkhill

Snail

First, a slippery face
It always seems to stay in the same place
It crawls, oh so slowly
With a hard shell on its back
It slithers and scurries
But I think it always hurries
Always late for dinner
Poor thing, never a winner!

Olivia Menmuir (8)
Birkhill Primary School, Birkhill

The Ladybird

This insect has spots,
And two wings.
It's not like a bee,
Or like a wasp that stings.

It is red and can fly,
Very, very fast.
If you look at it,
It will zoom right past.

Hannah Stewart (9)
Birkhill Primary School, Birkhill

Through That Door

Through that door
is a high wall
surrounded with flowers
that grow so tall
where a castle stands
that holds a princess
with long smooth hair
who is still in that castle today
climbing a million stairs.

That's what I saw
Through that door.

Verity Marshall (8)
Birkhill Primary School, Birkhill

Midge

Bites your head
Becomes a spot
Very itchy.
Tiny to see
Up in the sky
Two wings on its back
But you can't see it fly.

Chloe Shaw (8)
Birkhill Primary School, Birkhill

The Ant

Crawls around and sometimes bites.
Very small with a colony.
Mostly lives under stones and slabs.
It loves to use leaves,
Making them mouldy for their nests.

Marnie Mollins (8)
Birkhill Primary School, Birkhill

There Once Were Three Little Pigs

There once were three little pigs
Who had three little kids.
They decided to leave home
And start on their own.
One made a house out of glass,
The other kids thought it was first class.
The second made a house out of straw
And the others thought it was a bit raw.
The third had no home at all
So that's how it ended after all.

Paul Smith (10)
Birkhill Primary School, Birkhill

The Daddy-Long-Legs

Out of the sky
There came an eight-legged insect.
It came
It landed on the grass.
It tucked in its wings
And started to hunt for smaller insects.

Lorraine Bailey (9)
Birkhill Primary School, Birkhill

Parrot

P arrots are very noisy.
A lso very colourful.
R ed and yellow and green and blue.
R aising their voices out loud.
O ut and about the garden.
T ugging at the rope outside with their strong beaks.

Lauren Doughty (8)
Birkhill Primary School, Birkhill

The Chimpanzee

In the old tree house
cold, wet, mossy
scoopy and eeky
lives a chimpanzee
swinging and friendly
swooping and looping
swaying from rope to rope
looking for food
that children left behind.

Emma Whitelaw (8)
Birkhill Primary School, Birkhill

Anger

Anger is like a volcano shooting lava.
Anger sounds like a volcano exploding.
It tastes like blood.
It smells like soup.
Anger looks like a T-rex.
Anger feels like rubber.
Anger reminds me of my brother.

Ryan Caffney (10)
Birkhill Primary School, Birkhill

The Chickens

Clucking around my garden
Holding onto their worms
I go every morning to let them out
Crows help to eat their bread
Killing little insects
Eating up all the corn
Never staying still.

Andrea Goodman (8)
Birkhill Primary School, Birkhill

Wings
(Inspired by 'If I Had Wings' by Pie Corbett)

If I had wings
I would glide in the wind
And go on holiday every day to France or Spain.

If I had wings
I would eat clouds like candyfloss
And if I liked them there would be no more more clouds in the sky.

If I had wings
I would touch the sky or go higher
And go into space and float.

If I had wings
I would race aeroplanes or rockets
And fly over rainbows.

Aaron Small (8)
Birkhill Primary School, Birkhill

Fox

I am a fox,
as swift as can be,
even my mother,
cannot find me.

When I am hiding,
behind a tree,
my stupid predator,
cannot see me.

But sometimes I wish,
I was not a fox,
it is like I am,
in a cardboard box.

When people see me,
they just run away,
even when,
I have something to say

Andrew Burr (9)
Blackhall Primary School, Edinburgh

Plankton

Light comes
light comes
shrinks to the
bottom. Night comes
night comes, goes
to the top. Bubble goes
pop! Whale charges . . .

. . . plankton runs back to the darkness
in the depth of the pool. The plankton
again feels safe . . . and cool.
He rushes looking for meals, he
shuffles the rocks and pushes the gravel
he doesn't stop
his endless search
for vital food. He
crawls under a cave . . .
he feels warm and happy
and falling
asleep
he
lies
down
and
a
light
comes
again.

Vincent Plummer (9)
Blackhall Primary School, Edinburgh

Rock Hyrax

They are really fluffy and really cute.
They can be really puffy or really scruffy.
They can be fast or really slow,
But they are happy where they go.

Grant McDonell (10)
Blackhall Primary School, Edinburgh

Cat

I am
hairy and
very scary
but only to
my prey, the
mouse
I sleep all
day and hunt
all night, for
my food, my
owners love me,
they groom me,
feed me and give
me cuddles, but
when none of
that is happening
I like
to sunbathe
in
the
hot
sun.

Laura Burt (10)
Blackhall Primary School, Edinburgh

Jellyfish

My stings can feel electric,
They shock again and again,
I can sting without knowing,
Creatures fear me,
I have no brain and can be very stupid,
I am a jellyfish.

Alex Larionov (9)
Blackhall Primary School, Edinburgh

Giraffe

A tall beautiful creature
Looks over the land
And eats from the thorn tree
Whilst standing on the sand
He said, 'It's fun to be so tall
Though sometimes I wish I were small.'

Campbell Orr (9)
Blackhall Primary School, Edinburgh

We Can Do Anything

We can do anything, you and me,
We can fly round the world, as you will see.
We'll fly round the world in one whole day,
And nobody will know that we've been away.
We can run four miles a day
And then the rest of the world will say . . .
'Come on! Come on! Come on!
You're nearly there,
Being able to do anything is extremely rare!'
We can do anything.
Do you know what this means?
We can do anything,
If we believe in our dreams.

Jessica Smith (8)
Chapel of Garioch Primary School, Inverurie

Boredom

Boredom is when you are sick.
Boredom is when you walk in the street.
Boredom is doing homework.
Boredom is when you are tired.
Boredom is when it is raining.

Daniel McNally (7)
Chapel of Garioch Primary School, Inverurie

My Cat Scooby

My cat Scooby is black and white,
And sometimes bites.
My cat is naughty,
And he uses a potty.
Likes to eat,
And there's nothing to beat
The taste buds in his mouth,
He crosses the road facing south.
My cat Scooby, he goes hyper,
And hisses like a viper.
When I watch TV eating my food,
He jumps on me like a bat.
I told you he was a naughty cat.

Dani Donald (8)
Chapel of Garioch Primary School, Inverurie

My Cat

My cat is sweet,
And likes pieces of meat.
He's black and white,
And sometimes bites.

He likes to drink out of any sink,
And he'll probably spill a pot of ink.
His name is Tumble and his tummy rumbles,
Plus he likes to play in the hay.

He has no tail just a stump,
He likes to play football with a peanut.
He likes to sleep on the mat,
Now you know more about my cat.

Beth Strachan (10)
Chapel of Garioch Primary School, Inverurie

Snow

I like playing in the snow
I like snow, it's such fun
I like making snowballs
I like making snowmen
I like it when the snow's so deep it makes my feet wet.

I like snow, it makes Christmas come
I like crunching through the snow
I like snow because it's cold
I like snow because I like making snow angels
I don't like it when there is none.

Ellen Robertson (9)
Chapel of Garioch Primary School, Inverurie

The Rain

When it rains I feel it's a shame,
It really is a pain,
I wish the rain would not be so vain,
When it's wet,
I have nothing to do but fret.

Stop the constant pest,
And let me rest,
Until it is dry,
I don't know why
I thought I'd be glad,
But I'm soon mad for a drink.

Kate Fowler (10)
Chapel of Garioch Primary School, Inverurie

Terrible Tanya

Terrible Tanya breaks every book,
She is so terrible you can't even look.

Terrible Tanya sets the carpet on fire!
Everybody says she is a liar.

Next day she snatches a paintbrush,
And says she's in a rush.

Terrible Tanya loves her dog.
Only joking! She'd rather collect logs.

Terrible Tanya shouts very loud,
Everyone thinks she's horrible but she's very proud.

One day she's on a boat,
She tips it over and comes out with a very wet coat!

Terrible Tanya strokes a cat,
But she can't resist hitting it with a bat.

Terrible Tanya is cutting things at her table
But decides to cut some cables.

So that is Terrible Tanya!

Tanya Gill (10)
Chapel of Garioch Primary School, Inverurie

Mountains

Mountains are high and reach up to the sky,
Their towering tops are made of sharp rocks,
This mountain is dressed in its best purple vest,
Only in the summer the birds come to nest,
Up above the birds are soaring,
Down below the rooks are cawing,
The howling wind is making me shiver,
Strange sounds are making me quiver,
I am never alone when I'm on this mountain,
Because this mountain is my home.

Bridie Pryce (9)
Chapel of Garioch Primary School, Inverurie

Don't!

Parents always say, 'Don't!', so why can't they say, 'Do?'

'Don't sing in the shower
Don't bounce on your bed
Don't touch the hot kettle
Don't stand on your head
Don't eat all the chocolate
Don't mess up your hair
Don't eat all the sweets
Don't shout at the mayor
Don't paint your face red
Don't bite your nails
Don't ride on your dog
Don't squash all the snails
Don't eat all the pork
Don't throw snowballs at signs
Don't break the armchair
Don't park on red lines
Don't rob the bank
Don't drive in the car
Don't smash the trash
Don't play your guitar.'

They all might as well say, 'Don't do anything!'

Michael Walls (9)
Chapel of Garioch Primary School, Inverurie

My Rabbit Lilly Eveonah Rose

My rabbit is cute and sweet,
She likes to eat,
She is beige-ish brown,
And has fluffy down,

She sometimes bites,
And occasionally fights,
But don't get me wrong . . .
Lilly loves me!

Jordan Ramsay (8)
Chapel of Garioch Primary School, Inverurie

Nightmare

Bedtime!
This word is horrible,
It makes me shudder,
It makes my heart run cold.
I try to put it off but finally,
I have to go up to my bedroom,
To my bed where I will rest my
Sleepy head . . .

I am scared up there alone,
Especially when I hear a drone.
Then my eyelids start to flutter
And my body goes into a restless slumber.
Full of darkness and monsters that eat . . .
Human flesh!

In my dreams I'm alone in the wood,
When out comes a figure in a blood-red hood.
He comes right up to me and starts to bite,
This gives me a terrible fright!

I wake with a start,
And start to scream.
It really was a terrible dream!
I crawl out of bed and go downstairs,
Then watch TV to get rid of my nightmares.

Kirsty Smith (9)
Chapel of Garioch Primary School, Inverurie

Rain

Rain, rain, oh what a shame
Why is it raining today?
Come on Cruella, get your umbrella
And sing out into the rain

Rain, rain, it's a boring day
Go away right now
Don't come back
Forever and ever
Then we will all be happy.

Rebecca Fyfe (9)
Chapel of Garioch Primary School, Inverurie

A Super Smasher

A super smasher
A fast dasher
A krill killer
A big pillar
A good burner
A bad turner
A huge tail
A powerful bail
A big bin.

A catalogue to make me a
Killer whale!

Benjamin Wong (10)
Edinburgh Academy Junior School, Edinburgh

Young Tom

There was a very young boy called Tom
Who liked to play with coloured pompoms
The pompoms were yellow
And that's why he bellowed
That very young playful boy called Tom.

Barney Withall (11)
Edinburgh Academy Junior School, Edinburgh

Pig Vader!

There was a tubby pig called Pie
Who wished he could be a Jedi
They gave him a lightsaber
And he became Pig Vader
That happy tubby pig called Pie!

Bill Thompson (10)
Edinburgh Academy Junior School, Edinburgh

Hallowe'en Cinquain

Today
It's Hallowe'en.
People in sheets, flying.
Next day is definitely my . . .
Birthday!

Marc Petrie (10)
Edinburgh Academy Junior School, Edinburgh

Archie

There was a wee dog called Archie
Who was lively and real sparky
He had a friend called Jed
Who lived in a big shed
That wee dog called Sparky Archie.

Ben Brown (10)
Edinburgh Academy Junior School, Edinburgh

Flying Pig

There once was a very fat pig
That wore a very handsome wig
It flew overhead
Whilst all were in bed
That chubby old pig with a wig.

Finn Macpherson (10)
Edinburgh Academy Junior School, Edinburgh

The Pig In A Wig

There was a pig who liked to wear wigs,
He loved singing and dancing the jig,
But he lost his wig,
While doing the jig,
So he stopped wearing wigs during jigs.

Rory Hardie (10)
Edinburgh Academy Junior School, Edinburgh

A Boy Who Wore Socks

There was a young boy who wore socks
He was playing with an old box
In that box he got stuck
He was covered in muck
There was a young boy who wore socks.

Ross Millican (11)
Edinburgh Academy Junior School, Edinburgh

The Fat Old Man

There once was a fat old man that stank,
It was from the rotten beans he drank,
He went to a pig farm,
A fat pig ate his arm
And that was the end of the fat man.

Ruaridh Gale (11)
Edinburgh Academy Junior School, Edinburgh

Tyree

There was an old hippo called Tyree
She liked to eat the elephant's tea
But sadly she was killed
Because she was too filled
That dear old full hippo called Tyree.

Nathaniel Brailsford (10)
Edinburgh Academy Junior School, Edinburgh

Mr Crab

A nasty clipper
A fast nipper
A sideways walker
A creepy stalker
A shell liver
A food giver
A velvet back
A loud crack

A catalogue to make me a crab!

Patrick Paterson (11)
Edinburgh Academy Junior School, Edinburgh

Vietnam Cinquain

Listen . . .
How I hate this
It's not the jungle sound
It's people dropping to the ground
Why, why . . . ?

John Smyth (10)
Edinburgh Academy Junior School, Edinburgh

The Clock

The clock has an eye looking down at us
The clock has two arms like you and me
The clock has a needle like a doctor's
The clock is black and white like a zebra
The clock has a face like me
The clock has numbers like a maths jotter.

Azeem Nabi (8)
Flora Stevenson Primary School, Edinburgh

School

School is good, school is fun
School helps people concentrate
We do our English and our maths
Walking down the learning path
The bell goes *bing,* it's time to go and
In my head there's more I know.

Alix Taylor (9)
Flora Stevenson Primary School, Edinburgh

Joy

Joy is yellow as the sun
It tastes like ice cream in the spring
It smells like flowers in the breeze
Joy looks like children playing
It sounds like people laughing
It feels like I've never been sad.

Peter Robertson (8)
Flora Stevenson Primary School, Edinburgh

Hatred

Hatred is dark as Hell,
As hot as a fiery furnace.
It is as damp as a cave,
It tastes bitter, not sweet.
It feels painful and it burns like fire.
It smells like rotten fish.
Anger
Is everywhere!

Michael Keegan (8)
Flora Stevenson Primary School, Edinburgh

Shaun The Shield Bug

When I think about Shaun the Shield Bug
It makes me want to put in an earplug
Because you see
I must agree
He has no musicality.

But now that I have seen
Such a lovely bug of green
I think that it was mean
Of me to say such a thing.

He is a lovely striped fellow
With a waist thin and narrow
So I hope he will forgive me
For my words so carefree.

Cara Targett-Ness (10)
Flora Stevenson Primary School, Edinburgh

Ladybug

There was a thing flying around me,
It was a ladybug, red and black.
What a lovely ladybug
Sat on a big leaf
But the ladybug began flying like a bird
And the ladybug never stopped.

Daphne Chi-Ching Leung (9)
Flora Stevenson Primary School, Edinburgh

Andrew Ant

I am Andrew Ant
I crawl around all day.
I crawl up people's legs
And I find it rather amusing.
But when the giant comes to scratch
I really have to dash!

Duncan Grant (9)
Flora Stevenson Primary School, Edinburgh

Colour Poem

The colour blue
Is like the colour of the sea
The sea is cool
It is the colour of the sky

The colour red
Is the best
It is in a red and yellow flame
That is very hot

The colour green
Is the colour of grass and fields
Which blow all the time
I like green
As it's the colour of a bean

The colour white
Is the colour of snow
You can throw snowballs
Go on your sledge
And go down a hill
Feel the wind blowing in your face

The colour yellow
Is the colour of a big hot flame
Burning higher and higher
Don't go near it
Or you will get burned.

Ross MacRae (9)
Kinneil Primary School, Bo'ness

Colour Poem

The colour red
Is like a tasty apple
Shining bright
With a crunchy bite

The colour green
Is like fresh-cut grass
And the horrible taste
Of Brussels sprouts
On Christmas Day

The colour blue
Is like the deep sea
With quite big fish
And a huge blue whale

The colour white
Is like the freezing snow
Fun to play in
Making snowmen

The colour yellow
Is like some cheese
I like to eat it
As a piece

The colour brown
Is like a strong horse
Jumping poles
In the muddy fields.

Jason Cochrane (9)
Kinneil Primary School, Bo'ness

Colours

The colour red is
The colour of a juicy apple
It is lovely red roses
And the colour of the burning hot fire

The colour pink is
The colour of really tasty candyfloss
It is a gorgeous pink limo
And the colour of cute little piglets

The colour blue is
The colour of the cute dolphin
It is the blue whale
And the very fun swimming pool

The colour green is
The colour of the frog
It is the green grasshopper
And the shiny apple

The colour yellow is
The colour of cheese
It is the yellow daffodil
And the golden sun

The colour white is
The colour of snow
It is clean white teeth
And the white roses.

Malcolm Thompson (9)
Kinneil Primary School, Bo'ness

Colours

The colour red
Is for blood in your body
The low glow in the sunset
When the roses bloom

The colour blue
Is for the bluebirds flying in the sky
Over the bluebells
And the aquarium
With a dolphin in a tank

The colour green
Is for the grass in the field
And grasshoppers on leaves
And flowers on stems

The colour white
Is for snow and frost in the winter
And the beautiful white clouds
In the blue sky

The colour yellow
Is for the nectar in a sunflower
In the yellow cornfields
And the pollen in the buttercup

The colour pink
Is for lipstick on lips
And candyfloss at a fair
And pigs on a farm.

Jordan Morris-Cromie (8)
Kinneil Primary School, Bo'ness

Colours

The colour red
Is the colour of flames glowing
The beautiful flames are glowing and flowing
Light in the dark night

The colour pink
Makes the boys wink
As the girl smiles
With pink lipstick.

The colour yellow
Is the colour of sweetcorn
Which babies are fed
When they are toddlers.

The colour green
Is the colour of stems
On beautiful flowers
Also the colour of a grasshopper
In the cornfields.

The colour blue
Is the colour of a dolphin
Or the colour of a bright blue sky
On a sunny day.

The colour white
Is the colour of a snowy swan
Or the colour of white snowdrops
In the lawn.

Taylor Greer (9)
Kinneil Primary School, Bo'ness

Colour Poem

The colour red is like juicy red strawberries
And a big red crunchy apple
Like some red-hot flames.

The colour blue is like the deep blue ocean
With little bluebirds flying by
When it is nice and hot
You pick some blueberries.

The colour green is like the bright green grass
Some juicy green grapes and lizards running by.

The colour white is like some fluffy white clouds
Or when you can't get to sleep
And you count some fluffy white sheep.

The colour yellow is like some yummy yellow cheese
Or honey straight from a bee
And a nice sunny day
At the yellow beach.

The colour pink
Is like some candyfloss at the fair
Or like nice pink bubblegum
Some pink gigantic pigs in the muddy fields.

Sophie Mill (9)
Kinneil Primary School, Bo'ness

The Blitz

Today
I can hear
Bombs hitting the ground
Like thunder in the sky

Today
I can smell
Fire from the building
Like my mum burning the toast

Today
I can feel
The vibration of the planes
Like a hammer hitting a piece of wood

Today
I can see
Flames from the buildings
Like a building falling

Today
I feel
I feel numb and scared.

Dylon Taylor (10)
Lynburn Primary School, Dunfermline

Destruction Of War

Today
I can hear
Bombs banging on the ground
Like feet stamping on the stairs

Today
I can smell
The gas from the bombs
It reminds me of sickness

Today
I can feel
The rubble banging off the shelter
Like rain on a windowpane

Today
I can see
Fire engines and the hose spraying water
Like rain falling from the sky

Today
Inside I feel sad and scared
As if I'm going to die.

Connor Whyte (10)
Lynburn Primary School, Dunfermline

War Cry

Today
I can hear
The guns firing bullets
Like a vibrating toy

Today
I can smell
The dust from the broken buildings
Like a sand blizzard in the desert

Today
I can feel
The coldness of the Anderson shelter
Like being in the water of the North Pole

Today
I can see
Nobody out in the street
Like walking into a ghost town

Today
Inside I feel
I'm going to die.

Keiran Millar (9)
Lynburn Primary School, Dunfermline

The Blitz

Today
I can hear
Guns firing bullets
Like thunder banging in the sky

Today
I can smell
Cigars from American soldiers
Like the chimney on a house

Today
I can feel
Dust from the houses
Like sand on the beach

Today
I can see
Smoke from the houses on fire
Like a burnt roast chicken

Today
Inside I feel
Like we should fight back.

Daniel Dow (11)
Lynburn Primary School, Dunfermline

The Blitz

Today
I can hear
The loud sirens
That hurt my ears

Today
I can smell
The fire
That hurts my throat

Today
I feel
Confused
'Cause I don't know what is going on

Today
I can see
Fire
In the distance

Today
Inside I feel
Empty.

Stephanie Caulfield (10)
Lynburn Primary School, Dunfermline

The Blitz

Today
I can hear
Bombs falling
Like a firework in the sky.

Today
I can smell
Smoke
Like a house is burning.

Today
I feel
Petrified
Like I'm shaking to death.

Today
I can see
People dying
Like a nightmare.

Today
Inside I feel
Like I am going to die.

Courtney Munoz (9)
Lynburn Primary School, Dunfermline

Destruction Of War

Today
I can hear
Bombs dropping from the planes
Like the waves crashing against the rocks

Today
I can smell
Fire from the flames
Like the smoke near to me

Today
I can feel
Coldness of the wind
Like the icy sea

Today
I can see
Smoke from the ground
Like the fire far away

Today
Inside I feel
An empty soul, like I have died.

James Davidson (9)
Lynburn Primary School, Dunfermline

How It Feels

Today
I can hear
Humming noises of planes
Flying fast across the sky

Today
I can smell
Lots of cigars being smoked
By American soldiers

Today
I can feel
The coldness of the wind
Like the icy sea

Today
I can see
Houses falling down
Like a nail getting hammered into the wall

Today
Inside I feel
Sympathy for those who have died
Like the end of the war.

Jade Robertson (9)
Lynburn Primary School, Dunfermline

How I Feel Now War Has Started

Today
I can hear
Someone screaming
Like someone scraping their nails on a chalkboard

Today
I can feel
My sister shaking
Like a volcano erupting

Today
I can see
Smoke from the fire
Like a burnt turkey

Today
I can smell
Cigars from the American soldiers of war
Like fire from the bombs

Today
Inside, I feel
My heart is empty.

Courtney Kirk (9)
Lynburn Primary School, Dunfermline

How I Feel Now War Has Started

Today
I can hear
Someone screaming
Like someone scraping their nails on a chalkboard

Today
I can feel
My sister shaking
Like a volcano erupting

Today
I can see
Smoke from the fire
Like a burnt turkey

Today
I can smell
Cigars from American soldiers of war
Like fire from the bombs

Today
Inside I feel
My heart is empty
Like there will never be love again.

Megan McCann (9)
Lynburn Primary School, Dunfermline

How I Feel

Today
I can hear
The people screaming
Like someone screeching on a bit of glass

Today
I feel scared
Like a rabbit
Stamping in his burrow

Today
I see buildings
Crashing down
Like dominoes

Today
I can smell dust
Like sand blowing on the beach

Today
Inside I feel
Like my heart is broken.

Jody Rogers (9)
Lynburn Primary School, Dunfermline

Trees Cinquain

Trees are
Red in autumn
Every tree has some buds
Each bud starts a leaf, seeds fall to
The ground.

Dale Scobie (11)
Newburgh Primary School, Newburgh

The Pain And Sorrow I Feel

(Dedicated to my dad)

Sitting beside him, waiting, praying,
That something,
Anything,
Will save him.
Alas, I try but I know he will die.
This pain inside, I remember . . . memories.
Happy, wonderful memories that tear through my heart
Like an arrow.
Memories of sailing through the sea,
Oh wow! my mum has caught the first fish!
I snap back into my ever-painful world,
And see him lying there,
Still.
His breathing more like rasping.
The pain in my heart is swelling,
Like a volcano ready to explode.
The tears that drip down from my face,
My family around me.
We just have to wait.

Samantha Cockburn (11)
Newburgh Primary School, Newburgh

The Giant

I've heard there's a giant in town!
He lives in that big house!
He's very clever, sharp and bright,
You can hear him a mile away,
With his voice so deep and loud!
They say he's a fussy eater . . .
No fruit or veg will pass his teeth -
Hey! Wait a minute, that sounds like *me!*

Jack Poolman (12)
Newburgh Primary School, Newburgh

The Stallion!

The stallion is galloping, so wild and free!
The stallion is free, as free as can be!

The mares all adore him, a leader he could be!
He stands tall and mighty,
Looks down on his herd,
For leader now is he!

When danger comes, he alerts his herd,
And they stampede away to safety!

He runs at the front of the herd!
For he is the leader,
The leader so wild and free!

Rachel Copland (11)
Newburgh Primary School, Newburgh

My Granny

Granny Rena was the best,
Better than all the rest,

I think about her every night
Can't stop crying of fright!

I think it's a bad dream
And that it will go away,
And that she will come back
Again
Some day!

Demi Carmichael (11)
Newburgh Primary School, Newburgh

My Mum

My mum is fantastic
She shows me how to love and care
And best of all
She is always there!

She wakes me up every morning
And drives me to school
I love my mum with all my heart
And I always will!

Jamie Gourlay (11)
Newburgh Primary School, Newburgh

Dream Holiday

Where is my dream holiday
The Caribbean, Spain, Australia or New Zealand?
Where the sun shines all the time?
Where it's cold and gloomy?
Oh, where is it?
Tell me! Tell me!
I'll fly around the world
To find my *dream holiday!*

Grace Trainer (12)
Newburgh Primary School, Newburgh

Friends For Life

Forever friends, Scott and Matthew
Running and playing all day along.

Every day talking and laughing
It will last for ever.

Scott and Matthew, best friends for life

And I mean it!

Scott Weir (11)
Park Road Primary School, Rosyth

Friendship

Me and my friend Gemma
always share funny jokes and secrets
and we talk to each other when we have problems.

Gemma and I don't talk about other people
and we try not to fall out
with anybody.

We always have lots of fun
when we are out
and we have lots of other friends
that we hang about with.

Gemma is just like a sister to me
because when I am upset
she is always beside me.

I am so glad I have Gemma as a friend.

Laura Taylor (11)
Park Road Primary School, Rosyth

The Greatest Friend Ever

My best friend and me never fall out,
Never hurt each other's feelings,
And never hurt each other physically.
We go well together.

OK, OK, so we do fall out,
But we always make up.
He is silly, sunny, sometimes snappy and snazzy.
He is silly a lot and sometimes gets out of hand,
Yet Hayden is still my best friend.

Connor Dewar (11)
Park Road Primary School, Rosyth

Friendship

A friend will always be there
If you're feeling down
They'll laugh at all your jokes
You'll be accepted for who you are
A friend can be trusted
To keep secrets that you share
You will always have someone to play with
To shout and muck around with

Friends will sometimes have a fight
And fall out forever
But mostly you'll be friends the next day
Friends will have some other people
Who they'll be mates with
It can leave you left out and upset
But really they're still your best friends

Everyone should have a best friend
If not, you will be lonely and sad
That's why they're in groups
Because they're
Best friends for life.

Todd Buttercase (11)
Park Road Primary School, Rosyth

Me And My Friend William

Me and my friend William
Share games all the time.
That's on Sunday.

We love to go up to the woods
And do things we shouldn't do,
Like going in people's gardens.
We play with his brother with toy guns.

We're like brothers, me and my friend William.

Connor Fraser (12)
Park Road Primary School, Rosyth

My Friend And Me

My friend and me
We have lots of fun
Hanging upside down
And all around

My friend and me
We laugh and giggle
Joking all day
And snoring all night

My friend and me
We argue and fight
Gossiping aloud
And making up in the end

My friend and me
We walk about
Finding out gossip
And what news is around

My friend and me
Are the bestest friends ever.

Rachel Ewan (11)
Park Road Primary School, Rosyth

My Best Friend

My friend always invites me to his house
My friend always helps me when I need help
My friend is always happy to see me
My friend is very reliable

We never lie to each other
We never disagree
We never annoy each other
We're like fire and wood.

Jamie Penman (12)
Park Road Primary School, Rosyth

My Best Friend

My best friend is called Rebecca
She has blonde hair
And blue eyes
We both have nicknames too
Mine is Ame and Rebecca is Becca.

It's strange the similarities we have
Like
Same glasses
Doing athletics
And singing along to 'Take That'.

It would be so weird if
Rebecca wasn't my best friend
Because we do almost everything
Together.

My best friend
Is like the other half
Of me
We are like twin sisters.

I am so glad she is my best friend.

Aimee Hynd (11)
Park Road Primary School, Rosyth

Emotion Poem

Happiness is as yellow as the sun
It feels like happiness is coming and going
It tastes like a butterfly flying in the sky
It reminds me of my hamster.

Love is red for a big love heart
It feels like love is coming near
It tastes like something tasty
It reminds me of my grandad.

Jennifer Cope (9)
Park Road Primary School, Rosyth

Friendship Poem

My friend Caitlin
Is a very good friend
She always laughs
And smiles.

She plays with people
And is very kind
Caitlin helps people
With things.

If you're bored
She will think of something
Caitlin is really friendly
And kind.

I talk to her on MSN
And stay at her house
I wish that we
Stay friends forever.

Micaela Brown (11)
Park Road Primary School, Rosyth

Me And My Friends

Me and my friends
Play games together
Share things with each other
Nearly every day.

Me and my friends
Have a laugh
We hardly ever fall out
And when we fall out
We make up again.

Me and my friends
Are like brothers
We stay over at each other's houses
And go on adventures.

Liam Sloan (12)
Park Road Primary School, Rosyth

Friends

A friendship is
Kindness
Loyalty
Caring for each other
Sharing
Looking out for each other
Generosity
Trying to sort out each other's problems
That's what Catriona and me have together

Our friendship is
Full of surprises
A happy friendship
A fun friendship
A loyal friendship
That's our friendship.

Amy Barbour (11)
Park Road Primary School, Rosyth

Friendship

Me and my friends
Always get along.
We tell each other secrets
And make each other laugh.
We always help each other if one of us is hurt.

We always have lots of fun
Playing football every day.
If one of us has a problem, we try to sort it out
And we always work as a group.

We sometimes argue and shout
But if we fall out with each other
We will be friends a couple of minutes later.

Me and my friends are the best of friends.

Kyle Thomson (12)
Park Road Primary School, Rosyth

Emotions Poem

Laughter:
Laughter has got lots of colours, like purple, red and blue.
It feels like a balloon has just gone *bong!* in your tummy.
Laughter looks like your eyes are going to pop out
And you are going to fall off your seat!

Scared:
Scared is all black and dark.
You feel like you are going to break down any minute.
It looks like you are going to faint and hide behind a pillow.
It sounds like someone screaming but it never goes away.

Love:
Love is the colours of pink and shiny gold.
You feel like you want to say something but then you freeze,
Then you feel really dumb.
It sounds like angels starting to sing, *la, la, la.*

Phoebe Barbour
Park Road Primary School, Rosyth

My Friend

My friend Sarah is
Kind and caring
Cheers me up when I'm down
And is always there for me.

We have our fall-outs
We argue and fight
But we make up in the end.

Friendship is a word
And my friend gives it a meaning.

My friend is great!

Zoe Drury (11)
Park Road Primary School, Rosyth

Emotion Poem

Excitement:
Excitement is a mixture of nice bright colours, like the rainbow,
It is like a new dog being born,
It tastes like a double chocolate ice cream cone being licked by my tongue,
It reminds me of going inside a limo to ride.

Scared:
Scared is a mixture of horrible colours like black, brown and grey,
It feels like having two big buffaloes bouncing up and down
in your tummy,
It tastes like a big lump of mouldy cheese being shoved
on your plate,
It reminds me of a bad dream I had that made me forget things.

Peace:
Peace is a warm, creamy, pinkish colour,
It feels like two big, soft pillows bursting out on your bed,
It looks pretty like pink candles and nice flowers
And reminds me of a sunny day.

Zoe Cook (9)
Park Road Primary School, Rosyth

My Best Friend

My best friend is Zoe
She is . . .
Kind, caring and helpful
She is always there when I am down.

We have our fall-outs
Our silly fights
But no matter what, we are still best friends.

'Best friend' is just two words
But Zoe gives them a meaning.

Zoe is just like a sister to me.

Sarah Pettiglio (11)
Park Road Primary School, Rosyth

Feelings

Anger:
Anger is as red as blood,
It sounds like a train engine burning,
It really feels like lava pouring through you,
Anger tastes like a fire on your tongue,
It reminds me of a volcano exploding.

Boredom:
Boredom is when you're as tired as a sloth,
Just sounds like *blah, blah, blah,*
It feels like going to sleep for 100 years,
It tastes like sweet toffee in your mouth,
It reminds me of going to sleep.

Curiosity:
Curious is lots of ideas rushing into your head,
It sounds like a voice telling you what to do, and you feel
                                        you've got to,
It tastes empty, trying to get something to taste,
It reminds me of my Easter egg hunt.

Alice Eve Roberts (9)
Park Road Primary School, Rosyth

Emotion Poem

Being scared is like a big thing coming up behind you with big fangs.
It has big feet and hands and long hair.

Sleepiness is softer than a big pillow.
It is as blue as the sky on a summer's day.
It sounds like a tiger roaring
If you've heard my dad snoring.

Happiness feels like a soft cloud.
It's as yellow as the sun.
It is bigger than the biggest bun.
I wish there were something called a happy gun.

Ross Galloway Stuart (9)
Park Road Primary School, Rosyth

Emotions

Peace:
Peace is the crystal-clear water rushing down the river.
Peace is the calm blue sky.
Peace is a relaxing day off.

Anger:
Anger is as red as blood pouring out of my brother's nose.
Anger is like a volcano exploding with lava running down.
Anger is the cry of battle beginning at dawn.

Loneliness:
Loneliness is the star in the sky shining brightly.
Loneliness is the last egg to hatch.
Loneliness is the colour white with no one else around it.

Happiness:
Happiness is a baby born into its mother's arms.
Happiness is a bird's song on a summer's day.
Happiness is a bright summer sun.

Sadness:
Sadness is the colour black.
Sadness is a baby's cries.
Sadness is being left alone in the woods at night.

Lindsay Smith (9)
Park Road Primary School, Rosyth

Happiness

Happiness is the colour of the sun,
Bright and colourful,
I hear the wind blowing in my car,
It feels like happiness is coming here,
You touch a flower, it makes you laugh,
I look at the stars, they remind me of my gran up in the sky,
I taste fruit, it makes me small like a little star,
Sparkling in the bright sky.

Kelsey Lenaghan (9)
Park Road Primary School, Rosyth

Feelings

Peace:
Peace is as blue as the sky
It sounds like water flowing down a stream
It feels like you're sleeping on a cloud
It tastes like candyfloss melting in your mouth.

Fun:
Fun is as bright as the sun
It sounds like people laughing
It feels like you're going to the fair
It tastes like dark chocolate mixed with nuts

Anger:
Anger is as red as blood
It sounds like a lion roaring for its mum
It feels like you've just been shot
It tastes like extra-hot sauce burning on your tongue

Scared:
Scared is as black as a haunted house
It sounds like someone screaming
It feels like someone is chasing you
It tastes like raw meat.

Catriona Kirk (9)
Park Road Primary School, Rosyth

Emotion Poem

Loneliness:
Loneliness is as blue as tears falling from your face.
You feel like you're the only one left in the universe.
You think that you are invisible and no one can see you.
It reminds me of my mum because I don't see her much.

Kiera Hynd (9)
Park Road Primary School, Rosyth

Emotion Poem

Sleepiness is as blue as a sky on a summer's day,
Sleepiness as soft as a pillow,
It looks like a nice hot summery day,
It feels like an ice lolly.

Anger is as red as blood,
A roaring tiger on the prowl,
It feels like a poison rushing through your body,
Tasting like extra hot sauce burning on your tongue.

Sadness is as dull as a miserable day,
It reminds me of a funeral,
It tastes like smooth yoghurt,
It feels like smooth lips,
Sadness looks like a red rose.

Laughter looks like the sun,
It makes you feel like you are going to fall off your seat,
Laughter has lots of colours, red, blue, green and purple.

Love is the colour of pink,
It feels like a pillow tapping on your head,
Love looks like a red flower,
It sounds like rain hitting the ground.

Laura Mackenzie (9)
Park Road Primary School, Rosyth

Friendship Day Poem

My friend, Gemma, always makes me laugh
She is always telling funny jokes
And always makes me smile.

She is always up for a laugh
Even when she is feeling down
We always tell each other our secrets and problems.

I know we sometimes have arguments and rows
But I know we will always be best friends forever
No matter what.

Claire Douglas (11)
Park Road Primary School, Rosyth

Emotions Poem

Happiness:
Happiness is yellow like the sun.
It looks like butterflies playing happily in the sky.
It feels like touching a warm and fluffy rabbit.
It tastes like a Twister ice lolly on a hot day
It makes you want to dance or play with someone.

Confusion:
Confusion is like a puzzle with ten million pieces and no pictures.
It looks like a wall with no end.
It feels like touching snow that isn't cold.
It tastes like warm grapes.

Anger:
Anger is as red as blood.
It looks like spiders and tarantulas.
It feels like extra-hot, hot, hot sauce on your tongue.
It makes you want to run under your bedcovers as it is really mean.

Sadness:
Sadness looks like rotten autumn leaves.
It feels like tears dropping on your hand.
It makes you want to cry.
It's like watching your life as it suffers from illness.

Love:
Love is like a bird landing on your shoulder.
It sounds like bells ringing.
It looks like mistletoe.

Excitement:
Excitement is like getting a present every day of the year.
It feels like a bit of plain paper.
It feels like a butterfly flying so close to you, you can feel its wings
brushing against you.

Chloe Sandilands (9)
Park Road Primary School, Rosyth

Emotions

Happiness:
Happiness is like a daisy bursting with life.
You touch happiness just like you're touching the sky.
Happiness is great, it rarely makes you cry.
If you feel happiness, you'll never want to run away!

Anger:
Anger is as red as blood.
It makes you feel like you want to chuck mud.
It sounds like a lion roaring inside your head.
You touch it like you're tasting a spicy curry.
It reminds me of when people have a tantrum.

Excitement:
Excitement makes you feel like you just can't wait.
You wriggle around, you can't stay still.
You're waiting for your new toy to get scanned at the till.
You ask and ask, 'Can we go?'
But the answer's always, 'No!'
When you get your new toy, it's exciting for a day,
Then the next day you'll say, 'I wish it were yesterday.'

Scared:
Being scared is dark and dull.
It's like a huge skull.
You want to scrunch up in a little ball and hide.
When you're scared, your teeth will show worriedly.
You hear weird noises inside your head.
Your face goes red, very, very red.

Sadness:
Sadness makes you feel like you want to burst out crying.
When you're sad, you give up, stop trying.
When you're sad, your tears make you look a state, it doesn't look
very great.

So try never to be sad.
It just feels so bad!

Megan Lister (9)
Park Road Primary School, Rosyth

Feelings

Anger is . . .
As red as a cherry tomato
It tastes like an extra-hot sauce burning all your taste buds
It feels like holly pricking your hand
It reminds you of people fighting

Peace is . . .
As white as snow
It feels like soft fluffy clouds
It reminds me of a very sunny day
It feels like very still water

Happiness is . . .
As colourful as the rainbow
As smooth as silk
It tastes like very icy orange juice
It looks like a huge smiling face

Depression is . . .
As black as coal
It tastes like disgusting medicine
It reminds me of unhappy faces
It feels like a brick weighing on your shoulders

Love is . . .
As pink as a rose on a summer's night
It tastes like strawberries with cream
It reminds me of kisses
It feels like a very soft cushion.

Lauren Howitt (9)
Park Road Primary School, Rosyth

Emotions

Confusion:
Confusion is as multicoloured as the big bright rainbow,
A murmur of voices going round and round in your head,
It feels like you are stuck in a howling wind tornado,
                              not able to jump out,
It tastes like out-of-date Rice Krispies with big brown lumps.

Happiness:
Happiness is as yellow as a new-grown sunflower,
It sounds like chirping birds in the blue sky,
It feels like sitting in a boiling jacuzzi,
It tastes like Cadbury's milk chocolate, melting in your mouth.

Anger:
Anger is as red as a fire engine,
It sounds like a siren or alarm going off in your head,
It feels like you are being poked by the Devil's fork,
It tastes like chilli with extra-hot sauce with no water to spare.

Boredom:
Boredom is like an old, fading grey pair of socks,
It doesn't sound like people saying, 'Hey, hey!'
It feels like you have been kicked in the bottom,
It tastes like a burnt burger in your little mouth.

Amy Deas (9)
Park Road Primary School, Rosyth

The Deadly Witch

In the forest lives an old hag,
Deep in the dark forest,
Her voice is cruel,
Her eyes like a ball of fire,
Her teeth like daggers,
Nails like an eagle's talons,
A revolting witch,
Chanting her vicious spell.

Kristofer Maitland (8)
St Andrew's Primary School, Fraserburgh

Medusa

Down, down deep in Canada
Where the lava fields are far away
From the city of Canbonya
Is the cave of the Gorgons
And one is Medusa
Her head is most disgusting
Because it is pulsing in verrucas
Ah! but her eyes glow like fire
In a hurricane, only darker
Her tongue is blood-red
Her body is monstrous
But that's not all . . .
If you look directly into her eyes
She'll turn you into stone
The noise she makes is terrible
It's like a dog's bark
And a snake's hiss all together
If she's looking for prey
Don't visit the Gorgons!

Marc Busby (9)
St Andrew's Primary School, Fraserburgh

Medusa

Medusa lives in her lair,
Her head is hideous,
Snakes are her hair.
Her eyes are like fireballs,
Her tongue flickering
Between her pointed fangs,
Her body covered in scales,
Medusa is searching for prey,
She can smell from miles away,
She sounds like a lion,
She is roaring!

Isla Sutherland (8)
St Andrew's Primary School, Fraserburgh

Medusa

Deep down inside a lair,
Lived the terrifying Medusa,
The lair that she lived in,
Was all mouldy
And rotten rats
Scampered around,
Water that dripped
To the ground,
Her body was all scaly,
Her tail coiled around her,
Her fangs, sharp,
Her tongue, swaying,
Snakes for hair,
Hissing!

She was making a hissing noise,
While searching for prey,
Her eyes were full of mischief,
Her red eyes,
With little balls of fire,
Her body, slimy and stinking.

Holly Milne (8)
St Andrew's Primary School, Fraserburgh

Medusa

Revolting, gasping
In her lair
Searching for prey
On her head, snakes all about
Not healthy
Her fangs like steel, metal and unbroken
Her body all scaly and spiked with scales
Her tail like a rattlesnake
Rattling all the time
Her eyes glowing in the dark
Her tongue like a snake's tongue.

Ross Lawrence (8)
St Andrew's Primary School, Fraserburgh

Medusa

Deep down
In a cave,
There lived Medusa,
Her cave was like a lair,
Her terrifying head
With snakes all round it,
Stone people all around,
Eyes like balls of fire,
Tongue hissing everywhere,
Like her hair,
Fangs black as coal,
Dreadful tail, all pointed,
Body no better,
Her noise disturbing
As she searched for her prey.

Nicole Ritchie (9)
St Andrew's Primary School, Fraserburgh

Medusa

Deep down in a very dark cavern,
Lived a hideous, terrifying animal,
Medusa.
Half-human, half-beast,
Her hair was snakes,
Her body was scales,
Her tail, gigantic and hideous,
And eyes even worse.
It was the horrible beast, Medusa!

Lara Reid (9)
St Andrew's Primary School, Fraserburgh

Medusa

Medusa lived
In a dark cavern
With broken bones
And water and sticky slime
Dripping down everywhere
And rats eating the bones . . .

Suddenly, there lying on the floor
Was Medusa with her red eyes
And she was lying down,
Her tongue forking about
And her fangs covered with blood
Dripping down
And her tail, pointed and sharp,
Her body, flat and very skinny.
Eyes to turn you into stone!

Stephanie Cardno (9)
St Andrew's Primary School, Fraserburgh

The Revolting Witch

A dreadful witch lived in a burnt-out tree,
Boiling her vile potions,
Hair like slithering snakes,
Eyes like balls of fire,
And a long and warty nose,
Teeth all broken and green,
Hands with long yellow nails,
A long black cloak,
With a steepled hat,
Alive with spiders!

Chelsea Wilkinson (9)
St Andrew's Primary School, Fraserburgh

Medusa

A cave,
Dark,
Full of rats,
Bones,
People's stone bodies,
A pool of blood!
And a monster called Medusa,
She has serpents on her head,
Eyes like fireballs that turn people into stone,
Tongue flickering up to her nose,
Fangs like daggers,
And bones stuck to her gums,
Body as scaly as a dragon,
Her tail like a golden bat,
Searching for prey,
She sounds like a 1,000 snakes,

Monstrous!

Craig Massie (8)
St Andrew's Primary School, Fraserburgh

Medusa

Deep below the ground,
Lives Medusa,
In her lair,
Her body is scaly,
The snakes on her head are hissing,
Her fangs as sharp as a sword,
Her eyes as red as Hell,
Her tongue flickering,
Her tail flickering,
She's searching for her prey.

Brad Lockyer (9)
St Andrew's Primary School, Fraserburgh

Medusa

Medusa lives in her lair,
Dark and mouldy in her lair,
Slimy little snakes in her hair,
Her eyes red,
Her tongue like a snake's tongue,
Her fangs as sharp as a sword,
Her body scaly,
Her tail scaly,
Staring with her eyes,
Turning things to stone,
Looking for her prey,
She sometimes
Eats them.

Carrie Scott (8)
St Andrew's Primary School, Fraserburgh

Medusa

Medusa's lair
Is dark and creepy,
Crawling with bats and rats,
Her head is swarming
With snakes hissing,
Her eyes red and on fire,
Her body green and horrible,
Her tongue pointed,
Her fangs with blood all over them
And as sharp as daggers,
Her tail scaly,
Searching for her poison.

Shaun Muir (9)
St Andrew's Primary School, Fraserburgh

A Never-Ending Life

Living is a never-ending life,
In a school called St Andrews,
Secretly, silently, stalked a wrinkly hag,
Casting spells and cursing people.
In her tower she lived,
Along with her familiar,
A cat with piercing eyes.
The crone herself was hideous,
A malicious crone with eyes as red as Hell.
Her voice loud and piercing,
Hair tangled like string,
Her nose like an owl's beak,
Her teeth stained and broken,
Her hands all twisted and revolting.
Beside her is her prized possession,
An old tattered broom,
As she yawns and falls into her 'grave' bed.

Liam Maitland (9)
St Andrew's Primary School, Fraserburgh

Medusa

Lying in her lair deep in the ground,
Her fangs as sharp as sharks' teeth,
Her eyes, red as blood,
Her head more hideous than anything in the world,
Her hair like slithering snakes,
Her tongue, a serpent's tongue,
Hissing with greed,
Her body, scaly in all ways,
Her tail, slithering around the lair,
Moving her head as she searches for prey.

Meagan Ewing (8)
St Andrew's Primary School, Fraserburgh

Medusa

Deep down,
In a lair,
There lived Medusa,
Her head was gruesome,
Her snakes hissed,
Eyes like fire and big,
Her tongue long,
Her fangs all bloodied,
Her tail long,
She was growling because
Someone was coming . . .

Claire Smith (9)
St Andrew's Primary School, Fraserburgh

In A Giant's Pocket

In a giant's pocket you might find:
Stoneybridge School,
Breakfast
(10 days old),
A giant rubber
(2m long),
A giant fly
(dead, obviously),
A computer
(a small computer)
A bloodstain
(or a blob of blood),
A burnt match,
A human hand,
A human head.

And that's what you might find in a giant's pocket.

Joseph MacInnes (8)
Sgoil Staoinebrig, Stoneybridge

Ten Things I Would Really Like To Be

The ten things I would really like to be are:

A doctor,
I could find cures for diseases.

A chef,
I might cook for the Queen.

A marine biologist,
I could swim with dolphins.

An MSP
I would do a lot of arguing,

A police officer,
I would catch a lot of criminals.

A dentist,
(My dad thinks I'm going to be a dentist).

A teacher,
Everyone thinks I'm going to be a teacher (but I don't).

A gardener,
I would design a lot of gardens.

An air hostess,
I would get free plane rides.

But right now, I think I'll be *magical marvellous me!*

Sarah MacInnes (12)
Sgoil Staoinebrig, Stoneybridge

Young Writers Information

We hope you have enjoyed reading this book - and that you will continue to enjoy it in the coming years.

If you like reading and writing poetry drop us a line, or give us a call, and we'll send you a free information pack.

Alternatively if you would like to order further copies of this book or any of our other titles, then please give us a call or log onto our website at www.youngwriters.co.uk

Young Writers Information
Remus House
Coltsfoot Drive
Peterborough
PE2 9JX

(01733) 890066